10 MINUTE SATs TESTS

GRAMMAR, PUNCTUATION AND SPELLING

AGES 9–10
YEAR 5

KS2

Scholastic Education, an imprint of Scholastic Ltd

Book End, Range Road, Witney, Oxfordshire, OX29 0YD

Registered office: Westfield Road, Southam, Warwickshire CV47 0RA

www.scholastic.co.uk

© 2018, Scholastic Ltd

2 3 4 5 6 7 8 9   8 9 0 1 2 3 4 5 6 7

British Library Cataloguing-in-Publication Data

A catalogue record for this book is available from the British Library.

ISBN 978-1407-17518-8

Printed and bound by Bell and Bain Ltd, Glasgow

Author
Shelley Welsh

Editorial
Rachel Morgan, Vicki Yates, Rebecca Rothwell, Suzanne Adams, Vivienne Powell

Cover and Series Design
Scholastic Design Team: Nicolle Thomas and Neil Salt

Cover Illustration
Adam Linley @ Beehive Illustration, Visual Generation @ Shutterstock

Contents

How to use this book

This book contains ten different Grammar, Punctuation and Spelling tests for Year 5, each containing SATs-style questions. As a whole, the complete set of tests provides full coverage of the test framework for this age group.

It is intended that children will take around ten minutes to complete each test. Each test is in two parts and comprises 11 or 12 grammar and punctuation questions and four spellings. For example, Grammar and Punctuation Test 1 and Spelling Test 1 make up one full test which should take ten minutes to complete.

Grammar and punctuation tests

Each test comprises 11 or 12 questions, which amount to 12 marks in total. Some questions require a selected response, where children select the correct answer from a list. Other questions require a constructed response, where children insert a word or punctuation mark, or write a short answer of their own.

Spelling tests

There are four questions in each test, which amount to four marks. Read each spelling number followed by *The word is...* Read the context sentence and then repeat *The word is...* Leave at least a 12-second gap between spellings. More information can be found on page 59.

The glossary on page 50 provides a useful guide to the grammatical terms that children need to be familiar with, as well as some terms that support a wider understanding of English grammar.

Test 1
Grammar and Punctuation

10 MINS

Marks

1. Underline the **adjective** in the sentence below.

Daniel gratefully drank the cold water.

1

2. Add a different **prefix** to each word below to form its opposite meaning.

_____obey

_____construct

_____understand

1

3. Complete the sentence below with an appropriate **subordinating conjunction**.

Rashid put his coat on _____ it had started to rain.

1

4. Insert two **commas** in the correct places in the sentence below.

We took our cameras a packed lunch some bottles of water and notebooks on the trip.

1

KEEP IT GOING!

10 MINS

Marks

5. Which sentence below is **punctuated** correctly?

Tick **one**.

I went to bed early – at 7 o'clock – as it had been a long, hard day. ☐

I went to bed early at 7 o'clock – as it had been a long, hard day. ☐

I went to bed early – at 7 o'clock as it had been a long, hard day. ☐

I went – to bed early at 7 o'clock – as it had been a long, hard day. ☐

1

6. Complete the sentence below with a **noun** formed from the verb <u>enjoy</u>.

Our family gets a lot of _____ out of trips to the countryside.

1

7. Tick the sentence that must end with an **exclamation mark**.

Tick **one**.

How long is it since I've seen you ☐

What a long time it's been since I've seen you ☐

When do you think I'll see you again ☐

Why don't we see each other more often ☐

1

Marks

8. Circle the **relative pronoun** in the sentence below.

The soup that Mum made was full of healthy vegetables.

1

9. Which sentence below is **punctuated** correctly?

Tick **one**.

My uncle (the musician is playing on stage) this evening. ☐

My uncle the musician (is playing on stage) this evening. ☐

My uncle (the musician) is playing on stage this evening. ☐

My uncle the musician is playing (on stage this evening). ☐

1

10. What type of word is <u>calmly</u> in the sentence below?

The teacher calmly asked the girl to tidy up the mess.

Tick **one**.

an adjective ☐

a verb ☐

a noun ☐

an adverb ☐

1

KEEP IT GOING!

Marks

11. Which **verb tense** is underlined in the sentence below?

While Sam <u>was eating</u> his lunch, Ushma read her book.

Tick **one**.

past progressive ☐

simple past ☐

simple present ☐

present progressive ☐

1

12. Circle **one** word in each pair to complete the sentences using **Standard English**.

You should **of** / **have** brought your waterproof coat with you.

We haven't brought **anything** / **nothing** to drink.

1

Well done! END OF GRAMMAR & PUNCTUATION TEST 1!

Test 2
Grammar and Punctuation

10 MINS

Marks

1. Which sentence below is a **statement**?

Tick **one**.

Don't forget to water the plants ☐

Do you have any spare pencils ☐

There are 30 children in our class ☐

What a lot of books you have ☐

1

2. Insert a **comma** in the sentence below to avoid ambiguity.

"I like cooking dogs and hamsters," explained Ty.

1

3. Circle the **relative pronoun** in the sentence below.

There is the boy who burst my balloon.

1

4. Which sentence is written in **Standard English**?

Tick **one**.

Bethany seen her brother in the park. ☐

Our teacher said we done very well in our test. ☐

I brought some cakes to school today. ☐

I should of tidied my room better. ☐

1

Marks

5. Which sentence shows that you are **most likely** to miss the concert?

Tick **one**.

I might miss the concert this evening. ☐

I shall miss the concert this evening. ☐

I could miss the concert this evening. ☐

I may miss the concert this evening. ☐

1

6. What is the **word class** of the underlined words in the sentence below?

After <u>a</u> huge gust of wind, <u>the</u> leaves began to fall off <u>the</u> trees.

Tick **one**.

past progressive ☐

adverbs ☐

verbs ☐

determiners ☐

1

KEEP IT GOING!

10 MINS

Marks

7. Which underlined group of words is a **subordinate clause**?

Tick **one**.

<u>As we walked through the woods</u>, we saw an owl sitting in a tree. ☐

<u>After breakfast</u>, I always brush my teeth. ☐

When Mum goes shopping, <u>she always buys me a treat</u>. ☐

In my class, <u>there are 30 children</u>, one teacher and an assistant. ☐

1

8. Rewrite the **verbs** in the boxes to complete each sentence in the **simple past tense**.

While I ＿＿＿＿＿＿＿ tennis yesterday, it ＿＿＿＿＿＿＿ to rain.

play

begin

Mia ＿＿＿＿＿＿＿ to Spain last summer.

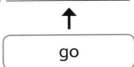

go

1

KEEP IT GOING!

Marks

9. Insert a **pair of brackets** in the correct place in the sentence below.

> We went to Paris the capital city of France for a long weekend.

1

10. Circle the **possessive pronoun** in the sentence below.

> I really like my brother's new bike but I think he prefers mine.

1

11. Complete the sentence below with a word formed from the **root word** <u>care</u>.

Zainab _____ mixed the flour and eggs.

1

12. Tick **one** box to show where the missing **comma** should go.

☐   ↓   ☐   ☐
                       ↓   ↓

> I am having cheese and cucumber sandwiches a yoghurt and an apple

1

Well done! END OF GRAMMAR & PUNCTUATION TEST 2!

Spelling test 1

Marks

1. My teacher asked me to _____ her to the library.

2. Mum _____ that we went to the park.

3. My favourite _____ is on TV tonight.

4. Padraig won the art _____ in our class.

4

Well done! END OF SPELLING TEST 1!

Spelling test 2

Marks

1. Our teacher said we could use a _____ to help us.

2. Freddy got a large _____ after he fell over.

3. We were very _____ when we saw the bull in the field.

4. We have been looking at the _____ ruins of Pompeii.

4

Well done! END OF SPELLING TEST 2!

Test 3
Grammar and Punctuation

10 MINS

Marks

1. Tick the sentence that must end with a **question mark**.

Tick **one**.

Pass me the books that are on the table ☐

Are there any more books on the table ☐

Jaime asked about the books on the table ☐

What a lot of books there are on the table ☐

1

2. Complete the sentence with an appropriate **adverb**.

The girls _____ worked out the answer.

1

3. Tick **two** boxes to show where the missing **inverted commas** should go.

If you tidy your room, we will go to the park, Bill's mum said.

↑ ↑ ↑ ↑

☐ ☐ ☐ ☐

1

4. Which sentence is a **command**?

Tick **one**.

Have you decided which book to read ☐

There are two halves in a whole ☐

How astonished I was to see my old friend ☐

Bring your bike into the garage ☐

1

Marks

5. Rewrite the underlined **verbs** in the sentence below so that they are in the **present progressive** form.

My mum <u>sits</u> in the shade while my brother and I <u>run</u> around.

↑   ↑

1

6. Which **verb form** completes the sentence?

After the farmer _____ the apples, he will store them in the barn.

Tick **one**.

have picked ☐

had picked ☐

has picked ☐

is picking ☐

1

7. Which sentence is written using **Standard English**?

Tick **one**.

The children was playing on the swings. ☐

Max done his homework quickly. ☐

There is a new film on at the cinema. ☐

We was listening carefully to the teacher. ☐

1

Marks

8. Complete the sentence below with an **adjective** derived from the noun <u>courage</u>.

The _____ knight chased the dragon into the cave.

1

9. Circle all the **prepositions** in the sentence below.

The bride and groom walked down the aisle and stopped under the arch.

1

10. Tick **one** box in each row to show whether the **apostrophe** is used for a contracted form or for possession.

Sentence	Apostrophe for a contracted form	Apostrophe for possession
What's happening after break?		
Tia has lost Liam's pencil case.		
I haven't seen Grace all week.		
Our teacher's chair is blue.		

1

KEEP IT GOING!

10 MINS

Marks

11. Write a **noun phrase** containing at least **three** words to complete the sentence below. Remember to punctuate your answer correctly.

_____ lives in a cottage by the sea.

_____

1

12. Draw lines to join each word to the correct **contraction**.

it is

it's

its'

would have

would'of

would've

1

Well done! END OF GRAMMAR & PUNCTUATION TEST 3!

Test 4
Grammar and Punctuation

1. Circle the **conjunction** in each sentence.

After we had finished eating, we all helped to wash up.

Beth likes tennis but she's not keen on badminton.

The school caretaker was brushing up the leaves as we left school.

1

2. What is the **function** of the sentence below?

The sprinter won his first gold medal

Tick **one**.

a question ☐

a statement ☐

a command ☐

an exclamation ☐

1

3. Which sentence is **punctuated** correctly?

Tick **one**.

We are learning about (World War I also known as the Great War) in history. ☐

We are learning about World War I (also known as the Great War) in history. ☐

We are learning about World War I also known as the Great War (in history). ☐

We are learning about World War (I also known as the Great War) in history. ☐

1

Marks

4. Which sentence uses the word <u>light</u> as a **noun**?

Tick **one**.

There was a light breeze blowing from the north. ☐

Dad switched the light off. ☐

Mum tried to light the bonfire with a match. ☐

My baby sister is as light as a feather. ☐

1

5. Complete the sentence below with a **verb** created from the adjective <u>intense</u>.

The atmosphere began to _____ as the athletes sprinted towards the finish line.

1

6. Complete the sentences below using the **simple past tense** of the **verbs** in the boxes.

Last summer, we _____ to France. We _____

↑

| go |

↑

| visit |

Paris and _____ the Eiffel Tower.

↑

| see |

1

Marks

7. Circle the **relative pronoun** in the sentence below.

There are many famous landmarks which I'd like to visit in London.

1

8. Which sentence is **punctuated** correctly?

Tick **one**.

We are going to the seaside today (unless it rains, of course). ☐

We are going to (the seaside today) unless it rains, of course. ☐

We are going to the seaside today (unless it rains), of course. ☐

We are going to the seaside today unless it rains, (of course). ☐

1

9. Circle the correct **verb form** in each pair to complete the sentences below.

Ben and Joe **done / did** their maths homework together.

Mum and I **is / are** going shopping later.

There **were / was** a big storm during the night.

1

KEEP IT GOING!

10 MINS

Marks

10. Rewrite the underlined **verbs** in the sentence below so that they are in the **simple past tense**.

[ ] ↓   [ ] ↓

Dad <u>drives</u> his new car to work every day. Mum <u>prefers</u> to take the train.

1

11. Insert two **commas** in the correct places in the sentences below.

After break our teacher usually reads us a story. Today the head teacher read to us instead.

1

12. Which sentence contains a **preposition**?

Tick **one**.

Grandpa likes baking sponge cakes. [ ]

Leah put the books on the shelf. [ ]

Will is still fast asleep. [ ]

Our car won't start. [ ]

1

Well done! END OF GRAMMAR & PUNCTUATION TEST 4!

Spelling tests 3 & 4

Spelling test 3

Marks

1. There was no _____ for the missing library book.

2. We went to a _____ to celebrate Mum's birthday.

3. I eat both fruit and _____ to keep me healthy.

4. Wahid banged his _____ playing rugby.

4

Well done! END OF SPELLING TEST 3!

Spelling test 4

Marks

1. Dad cooked an _____ stew.

2. The children waited for ages in the _____ .

3. We took out the climbing _____ in PE today.

4. Florence is a member of the school safety _____ .

4

Well done! END OF SPELLING TEST 4!

Marks

1. Circle two **adverbials** in the sentence below.

Later on, we are going to visit our cousins who live nearby.

1

2. Which sentence below contains a **relative pronoun**?

Tick **one**.

We will go outside when it stops raining. ☐

Mum, who was really handy, built a go-cart. ☐

My stepdad likes cooking whereas my
brother likes gardening. ☐

Kyron needs to finish his homework
before he goes out. ☐

1

3. Draw a line to match each word to the correct **suffix** to make an **adjective**.

Word	Suffix
thank	al
danger	ous
temperament	ful

1

4. Circle the word in the sentence that uses an **apostrophe** to show a missing letter.

Bavini's desperate to show us the new coat that her mum's friend
bought her.

1

23

10 MINS

5. Which sentence is an **exclamation**?

Tick **one**.

What an amazing garden you have ☐

What type of plant is that ☐

Why don't we feed the fish in the pond ☐

Pass me the fish food ☐

1

---

6. Rewrite the **verbs** in the boxes to complete each sentence with the correct choice of **tense**.

Sam always _____ his lunch with Hiro.

↑

| eat |

Our friends went home after they _____ the film.

↑

| watch |

1

KEEP IT GOING!

Marks

7. Tick **two** boxes to show where the missing **pair of commas** should go.

There are lots of children in my dance class 20 to be exact and

☐ ☐ ☐

we all get along very well.

☐

1

8. Add a word that belongs to the **word family** below.

circus	circumference	circular	

1

9. Tick **one** box in each row to show whether the underlined words are a **main clause** or a **subordinate clause**.

Sentence	Main clause	Subordinate clause
<u>If the weather improves,</u> we can go for a picnic.		
When the bell rings, <u>the children line up calmly.</u>		
There are three library books <u>that need to be returned.</u>		

1

Marks

10. Which sentence uses **capital letters** correctly?

Tick **one**.

Mr singh, our new teacher, makes us laugh. ☐

Year 5 is going to the museum on wednesday. ☐

We had a boat trip on the River Thames. ☐

Maisie read a book about Kangaroos and Koalas. ☐

1

11. a. Write a sentence using the word <u>tie</u> as a **verb**. Do not change the word. Remember to punctuate your sentence correctly.

_____

_____

1

b. Write a sentence using the word <u>tie</u> as a **noun**. Do not change the word. Remember to punctuate your sentence correctly.

_____

_____

1

Well done! END OF GRAMMAR & PUNCTUATION TEST 5!

Test 6
Grammar and Punctuation

10 MINS

Marks

1. Which sentence is a **command**?

Tick **one**.

Your homework is written on the board ☐

Hand in your homework ☐

Have you finished your homework ☐

How many pages have you written ☐

1

2. Insert **full stops** and **capital letters** in the passage below so that it is punctuated correctly.

In the summer holidays, I like going to the seaside while we are there, we usually visit my grandparents who have a caravan nearby it's even better if the sun is shining

1

3. Circle the correct **verb form** in each pair to complete the sentences below.

Last week, we **climbed / climb** to the top of the hill.

They usually **eat / are eating** cereal and toast for breakfast.

Yesterday, I **am swimming / was swimming** in a competition.

1

KEEP IT GOING!

4. Replace the underlined words in the sentence below with a **pronoun**.

Marks

When I had finished the book, I took <u>the book</u> to the library.

↑

1

---

5. Change the words below into **adverbs** by adding the suffix 'ly'. You may need to remove or change a letter.

love   _____

horrible   _____

hungry   _____

1

---

6. Which **verb form** completes the sentence below?

After we _____ the classroom, we went out to play.

Tick **one**.

had tidied   ☐

have tidied   ☐

are tidying   ☐

were tidying   ☐

1

Marks

7. Which sentence is punctuated correctly?

Tick **one**.

My sister Scarlet who only (yesterday stubbed her toe) has just fallen off the trampoline. ☐

My sister Scarlet who only yesterday stubbed her toe (has just fallen off the trampoline.) ☐

My sister Scarlet (who only yesterday stubbed her toe) has just fallen off the trampoline. ☐

My sister (Scarlet who only yesterday stubbed her toe) has just fallen off the trampoline. ☐

1

8. Which sentence uses **Standard English**?

Tick **one**.

My friend seen me in the cinema. ☐

We could of gone together. ☐

Mum's picking me up in her car. ☐

She done her shopping. ☐

1

9. Label each of the clauses in the sentence below as either **main (M)** or **subordinate (S)**.

The bell rang, which meant it was time to stop,

☐   ☐

but we were quite happy to carry on.

☐

1

Marks

10. Which **punctuation mark** should be used in the place indicated by the arrow?

↓

Where are the girls shoes?

Tick **one**.

comma ☐

question mark ☐

apostrophe ☐

hyphen ☐

1

11. a. Underline the **possessive pronoun** in the sentence below.

Wahid has lost his pen but Archie says he can borrow his.

1

b. What does the **possessive pronoun** refer to in this sentence?

Tick **one**.

Wahid ☐

Archie ☐

Wahid's pen ☐

Archie's pen ☐

1

Well done! END OF GRAMMAR & PUNCTUATION TEST 6!

10 MINS

Spelling test 5

Marks

1. We had a _____ trip to the farm.

2. My dad's _____ is firefighter.

3. We _____ lined up when the alarm sounded.

4. Our parents are celebrating _____ wedding anniversary.

4

Well done! END OF SPELLING TEST 5!

Spelling test 6

Marks

1. Dad was _____ he would scratch his new car.

2. There was a _____ sound coming from outside.

3. Aunty Liz checked the _____ of flights to Ireland.

4. I was _____ to get my spellings correct.

4

Well done! END OF SPELLING TEST 6!

Marks

1. Rearrange the words in the **statement** below to make it a **question**. Use only the given words. Remember to punctuate your sentence.

Statement: Bill is walking his dog.

Question: _____

1

2. Tick **one** box in each row to show whether the **commas** are used correctly in the sentence.

Sentence	Commas used correctly	Commas used incorrectly
We are having fish, chips, and peas tonight.		
My dog, whose name is Benji, is three today.		
Our history teacher explained the reasons, why World War II, began.		
The fire, which destroyed the forest area, has been extinguished.		

1

3. Underline the **relative clause** in the sentence below.

The floods that followed the storms have destroyed many homes.

1

32

Marks

4. Circle the **two** words that show the **tense** in the sentence below.

> Our school has a great reputation for sports and we win most competitions.

1

5. Replace the underlined words in the sentence with the correct **possessive pronoun**.

That pen belongs to <u>my brother</u>. That pen is _____.

1

6. Which sentence is **punctuated** correctly?

Tick **one**.

All over, the world, there is evidence of dinosaur footprints. ☐

All over the world, there is evidence of dinosaurfootprints. ☐

All over the world there is evidence, of dinosaur footprints. ☐

All over the world, there is evidence of, dinosaur footprints. ☐

1

Marks

7. What is the **word class** of the underlined words in the sentence below?

Dad was <u>exhausted</u> after carrying the <u>heavy</u> box.

Tick **one**.

adverbs ☐

determiners ☐

nouns ☐

adjectives ☐

1

8. Insert two **commas** in the sentence below to avoid ambiguity.

Mary Jane thinks is going to be late.

1

9. What is the **function** of the underlined words in the sentence below?

<u>A pretty, delicate butterfly</u> fluttered onto my arm.

Tick **one**.

expanded noun phrase ☐

subordinate clause ☐

main clause ☐

fronted adverbial ☐

KEEP IT GOING!

1

Marks

10. Tick the sentence where the **tense** is consistent.

Tick **one**.

We went to the museum and see a mammoth's skeleton. ☐

Dad wasn't feeling well so I help him tidy up. ☐

Gus ate his vegetables although he didn't really like them. ☐

After I had finished chopping the fruit, I make a smoothie. ☐

1

11. Add a **prefix** to the word <u>write</u> to make a word that means 'to write again'.

_____write

1

12. Add a **suffix** to the adjective <u>delicate</u> to form an adverb.

_____

1

Well done! END OF GRAMMAR & PUNCTUATION TEST 7!

Test 8
Grammar and Punctuation

10 MINS

Marks

1. Circle the two **conjunctions** in the sentence below.

Matthew likes carrots and peas but he doesn't like cauliflower.

1

2. Draw a line to match each sentence to its correct **function**. Use each function only **once**.

Sentence

We have been learning about ancient Greece

What have you learned about ancient Greece

What a lot we have learned about ancient Greece

Read this book about ancient Greece

Function

command

statement

question

exclamation

1

3. Insert one **comma** in the correct place in the sentence below.

With only two minutes to go it was clear who would win the race.

1

KEEP IT GOING!

10 MINS

Marks

4. Which **verb form** completes the sentence below?

As we _____ to school, we saw our friends Natasha and Sam.

Tick **one**.

were driving	☐
are driving	☐
had driven	☐
have driven	☐

1

5. You are helping a friend to correct the punctuation in the box below. Which **one** piece of advice should you give her?

The childrens shoes were lined up on the mat.

Tick **one**.

There should be an apostrophe after the 's' in 'childrens'. ☐

There should be an apostrophe after the final 's' in 'shoes'. ☐

There should be an apostrophe between the 'n' and the 's' in 'childrens'. ☐

There should be an apostrophe between the 'e' and the 's' in 'shoes'. ☐

1

KEEP IT GOING!

6. Underline the **subordinate clause** in the sentence below.

Remi did well in the maths test, even though he found it difficult.

Marks

1

7. Change each word below into a **verb** by adding an appropriate **suffix** from the box. Write the new word on the line.

ate	ise	ify

class _____

design _____

advert _____

1

8. Which sentence is written in **Standard English**?

Tick **one**.

Joe's done lots of hard work today. ☐

Look at them cakes! ☐

We should of invited Clare to the party. ☐

She hasn't got no pencils. ☐

1

9. Circle the two **adverbs** in the sentence below.

Luckily, Ted had worked hard on his times tables.

1

Marks

10. Which sentence is **punctuated** correctly?

Tick **one**.

Mum's brother – the one who lives in South Africa – is staying with us for a fortnight. ☐

Mum's brother the one – who lives in South Africa – is staying with us for a fortnight. ☐

Mum's brother the one who lives – in South Africa – is staying with us for a fortnight. ☐

Mum's brother the one who lives in South Africa – is staying with us – for a fortnight. ☐

1

11. Circle the correct **verb form** in each pair to complete each sentence below.

There **was / were** lots of people waiting in the queue.

They **was / were** cheering the winning team.

1

12. Circle the **relative pronoun** in the sentence below.

There's the team that won the winners' trophy.

1

Well done! END OF GRAMMAR & PUNCTUATION TEST 8!

Spelling test 7

Marks

1. It is _____ to eat a balanced diet.

2. Ben _____ to open his birthday present.

3. We gave the garage a _____ tidy.

4. I put the invitation in a white _____ .

4

Well done! END OF SPELLING TEST 7!

Spelling test 8

Marks

1. Petra _____ PE on the playing field.

2. Our _____ has two dogs and a cat.

3. Mum is _____ next year.

4. We visited the medieval _____ on the hill.

4

Well done! END OF SPELLING TEST 8!

Marks

1. Insert the missing **apostrophe** in each of the underlined words in the passage below.

Two days ago, my brother went to <u>Fayes</u> house for lunch and they had cheese and biscuits. <u>Its</u> my turn to go tomorrow.

1

2. Circle the **three determiners** in the sentence below.

Sonny cut up the cake and gave everyone an enormous slice and a drink.

1

3. Add a suitable word to the **word family** below.

| real | unreal | reality | |

1

4. Replace the underlined words in the sentence below with their **expanded forms**.

I've been looking forward to the trip to the park all day, so <u>I'm</u> a bit disappointed that <u>it's</u> started to rain.

1

5. Which sentence below is an **exclamation**?

Tick **one**.

How wonderful to see you at last ☐

You look just the same ☐

How many years has it been since I have seen you ☐

Let's have a look at some photographs ☐

Marks

1

---

6. Which sentence is written in **Standard English**?

Tick **one**.

We haven't got no good books. ☐

Did you bring them biscuits with you? ☐

He were there yesterday. ☐

I really admire the player who scored. ☐

1

---

7. Complete the sentence below with the **simple past tense** of the verb in the box.

We _____ to the cinema last night.

↑

go

1

KEEP IT GOING!

42

Marks

8. Tick the option that correctly completes the sentence below.

_____ started to bloom in Dad's flowerbed.

Tick **one**.

In the middle, of February, the daffodils ☐

In the middle of February the daffodils, ☐

In the middle of February, the daffodils ☐

In the middle of, February the daffodils ☐

1

9. Circle the correct spelling from the pair of **homophones** to complete the sentence below.

The children had just finished **their / there** test when the fire alarm sounded.

1

10. Circle the **pronoun** in the sentence below.

The dog was wet so Carl dried him with a towel.

1

KEEP IT GOING!

43

Marks

11. Which **punctuation mark** should be used in the place indicated by the arrow?

My dog Kip, who was always getting into mischief lost his ball in the park. ↑

Tick **one**.

a question mark ☐

a full stop ☐

a comma ☐

a bracket ☐

1

12. Rewrite the sentence below so that it starts with the **subordinate clause**. Remember to punctuate your answer correctly.

We went for a picnic although it was threatening to rain.

_____

_____

1

Well done! END OF GRAMMAR & PUNCTUATION TEST 9!

Marks

1. Circle the **relative pronoun** in the sentence below.

Great white sharks, which are grey with a white underbelly, can swim at over 60km per hour.

1

2. Which sentence uses **brackets** correctly?

Tick **one**.

My cousin (Sam always full of determination and courage) climbed to the top of Mount Snowdon. ☐

My cousin Sam (always full of determination and courage) climbed to the top of Mount Snowdon ☐

My cousin Sam always full of determination and courage climbed to the top of (Mount Snowdon ☐

My cousin Sam (always full of determination) and courage climbed to the top of Mount Snowdon. ☐

1

3. Which underlined group of words is a **relative clause**?

Tick **one**.

We always bring our camera when we go on holiday. ☐

There are still some children who have yet to finish. ☐

Although it's a drizzly morning, the forecast is good for later. ☐

My best friend Amie is having a party this weekend. ☐

1

45

Marks

4. Which sentence shows that you are most likely to visit your aunt at the weekend?

Tick **one**.

I shall visit my aunt at the weekend. ☐

I might visit my aunt at the weekend. ☐

I should visit my aunt at the weekend. ☐

I can visit my aunt at the weekend. ☐

1

5. Tick **one** box in each row to show whether the underlined words are a **main clause** or a **subordinate clause**.

Sentence	Main clause	Subordinate clause
After she had practised for months, <u>Charlie was able to play the piano beautifully</u>.		
<u>After they have walked to school,</u> Keir and Mollie have rosy cheeks.		
If I am struggling with my homework, <u>my stepdad helps me</u>.		

1

KEEP IT GOING!

Marks

6. Rearrange the words in the **statement** below to make it a **question**. Use only the given words. Remember to punctuate your sentence correctly.

Statement: Carmen was late today.

Question: _____

_____

1

7. Circle the **subordinating conjunction** in the sentence below.

Dad said we could watch the film if we helped to make dinner.

1

8. Which sentence is **punctuated** correctly?

Tick **one**.

"Who is coming outside to play?" Shouted Amir. ☐

"Who is coming outside to play"? shouted Amir. ☐

"Who is coming outside to play" shouted Amir? ☐

"Who is coming outside to play?" shouted Amir. ☐

1

9. Draw a line to match each word to the correct **suffix** to make a **noun**.

Word	Suffix
assist	ence
expect	ant
refer	ation

1

Marks

10. Complete the sentence below by writing the **conjunctions** from the boxes in the correct places. Use each conjunction only **once**.

| or | but | and |

There were baubles _____ lights on the tree, _____

Mum still hadn't added any tinsel _____ a fairy.

1

11. Tick **two** boxes to show where the missing **inverted commas** should go.

☐
↓

Today we are going to investigate animal habitats and adaptation, our teacher said.

↑ ↑ ↑
☐ ☐ ☐

1

12. Write a **noun phrase** containing at least **three** words to complete the sentence below.

Through his telescope, Finlay could see _____

_____ .

1

Well done! END OF GRAMMAR & PUNCTUATION TEST 10!

Spelling tests 9 & 10

Spelling test 9

Marks

1. Dad has been _____ to a different factory.

2. Our last spelling test was _____ but fair.

3. The yacht sailed towards the _____ in the distance.

4. We watched the spider crawl across the _____ .

4

Well done! END OF SPELLING TEST 9!

Spelling test 10

Marks

1. The _____ little puppy chewed Mum's slippers.

2. Jim was _____ with his science experiment.

3. We always get a _____ in the January sales.

4. Mo sometimes _____ how hungry he is.

4

Well done! END OF SPELLING TEST 10!

Grammar glossary

The 'Top ten trickiest terms' you should know

1. Noun phrase

A <u>noun phrase</u> is a group of words that provides more information about a noun. The **noun** is the most important word in the phrase.

That **dog**.
Those **people**.

A <u>noun phrase</u> can be expanded so that there is even more information about the noun.

That scruffy **dog**.
Those **people** with the funny hats.

2. Determiner

A <u>determiner</u> indicates whether a noun is specific/known (such as 'the', 'that', 'those') or more general/unknown (such as 'some', 'a').

<u>Those</u> children have left <u>some</u> rubbish next to <u>the</u> field.

3. Fronted adverbial

An adverbial is a word or phrase that describes when, how or where something is taking place. A <u>fronted adverbial</u> comes at the front of the sentence and is followed by a comma.

<u>In the morning,</u> we are going on holiday to France.

4. Perfect tense

The <u>perfect tense</u> is used to describe something that took place in the past. The <u>present perfect tense</u> describes something that began in the past but may still continue into the present. The **past perfect tense** describes something that occurred before another action in the past.

I <u>have worked</u> at the hospital for two years.
She **had fallen** asleep before the film started.

5. Progressive tense

The <u>progressive tense</u> usually describes events that are in progress (<u>present progressive</u>) or were in progress (**past progressive**).

Emma <u>is jumping</u> in the puddles.
Will **was speaking** to the teacher.

6. Exclamation sentences

An <u>exclamation sentence</u> starts with 'what' or 'how', contains a verb (otherwise it wouldn't be a sentence!) and ends with an exclamation mark.

<u>What a strange day it has been!</u>
<u>How clever that old man is!</u>

7. Modal verb

A <u>modal verb</u> goes before another verb to show how possible, certain or necessary something is.

The weather <u>may</u> turn colder next week.
Grandad <u>should</u> arrive home before Thursday.
You <u>must</u> finish your peas before you have a pudding.

8. Subordinating conjunction

A <u>subordinating conjunction</u> is a linking word or phrase. It links a subordinate clause to a main clause. The **subordinate clause** can come at the start, the middle or the end of a sentence. If it comes at the start of the sentence, it is followed by a comma.

I put on my coat **after** I had packed my bag.
After I had packed my bag, I put on my coat.

9. Parenthesis

A <u>parenthesis</u> is additional information inserted into a sentence. It is separated from the rest of the sentence by a pair of commas, brackets or dashes. You can remove a parenthesis and the sentence will still make sense.

My brother Sam – <u>the well-known musician</u> – is performing on TV tonight.
Last week, my aunt won a big prize in the lottery (<u>over £1000</u>).
Our grandparents, <u>usually fit and well,</u> are a bit under the weather.

10. Ambiguity

Ambiguity means having more than one possible meaning. Placing commas correctly can avoid ambiguity.

"Let's eat Uncle Harry!" shouted Ben.
"Let's eat, Uncle Harry!" shouted Ben.

Q	Mark scheme for Grammar and Punctuation Test 1	Marks
1	**Award 1 mark** if 'cold' is underlined. **Grammar essentials:** An adjective can come before a noun, to modify it.	1
2	**Award 1 mark** if all are correct: disobey, deconstruct, misunderstand. **Grammar essentials:** A prefix is added to the beginning of a word to turn it into another word. Some prefixes can be added to form the opposite meaning. A prefix does not alter the spelling of the word it is joined to.	1
3	**Award 1 mark** for either 'because', 'as' or 'since'. For example: Rashid put his coat on **because** it had started to rain. **Grammar essentials:** A subordinating conjunction (here 'because') introduces a subordinate clause (here 'it had started to rain.'). A subordinate clause will not make sense on its own	1
4	**Award 1 mark** for **two** commas correctly placed: We took our cameras, a packed lunch, some bottles of water and notebooks on the trip. **Grammar essentials:** Commas can be used to separate items in a list. Commas are used when there are more than two list items.	1
5	**Award 1 mark** if 'I went to bed early – at 7 o'clock – as it had been a long, hard day.' is ticked. **Punctuation essentials:** A pair of dashes can be used to indicate parenthesis. When you take the words in parentheses out of the sentence, the rest of the sentence makes sense on its own.	1
6	**Award 1 mark** for 'enjoyment', spelled correctly. **Grammar essentials:** Adding a suffix to some verbs can turn them into nouns.	1
7	**Award 1 mark** if 'What a long time it's been since I've seen you' is ticked **Grammar essentials:** An exclamation sentence starts with 'what' or 'how', contains a verb (otherwise it wouldn't be a sentence!) and ends with an exclamation mark.	1
8	**Award 1 mark** if the word 'that' is circled. **Grammar essentials:** The relative pronouns 'that', 'which', 'who', 'when', 'where' and 'whose' introduce a relative clause. They refer back to a noun or noun phrase that has come before.	1
9	**Award 1 mark** if 'My uncle (the musician) is playing on stage this evening.' is ticked. **Punctuation essentials:** A pair of brackets can be used to indicate parenthesis. When you take the words in parentheses out of the sentence, the rest of the sentence makes sense on its own.	1
10	**Award 1 mark** if 'an adverb' is ticked. **Grammar essentials:** An adverb can say how something happens. Remember, not all adverbs end in 'ly' and not all words ending in 'ly' are adverbs!	1
11	**Award 1 mark** if 'past progressive' is ticked. **Grammar essentials:** The past progressive tense describes events in the past that were continuous.	1
12	**Award 1 mark** if both 'have' and 'anything' are circled. **Grammar essentials:** 'We haven't brought nothing' would be a double negative, which is non-Standard English (grammatically incorrect). The use of 'of' instead of 'have' in constructions such as 'should have' and 'could have' is a common error caused by people writing what they hear.	1
	Total	12

Q	Mark scheme for Grammar and Punctuation Test 2	Marks
1	**Award 1 mark** if 'There are 30 children in our class' is ticked. **Grammar essentials:** A statement is a sentence that provides information.	1
2	**Award 1 mark** for a comma correctly placed: "I like cooking, dogs and hamsters," explained Ty. **Punctuation essentials:** Commas can be used to avoid ambiguity, as well as to separate items in a list.	1

Q	Mark scheme for Grammar and Punctuation Test 2	Marks
3	**Award 1 mark** for 'who' circled. **Grammar essentials:** The relative pronouns 'that', 'which', 'who', 'when', 'where' and 'whose' introduce a relative clause. They refer back to a noun or noun phrase that has come before.	1
4	**Award 1 mark** if 'I brought some cakes to school today.' is ticked. **Grammar essentials:** In Standard English, we use correct grammar.	1
5	**Award 1 mark** if 'I shall miss the concert this evening.' is ticked. **Grammar essentials:** The modal verb ('shall') goes before another verb to show how certain something is.	1
6	**Award 1 mark** if 'determiners' is ticked. **Grammar essentials:** A determiner is a word that goes before a noun, such as 'a', 'the', 'some', 'this' or 'my'.	1
7	**Award 1 mark** if the sentence '<u>As we walked through the woods</u>, we saw an owl sitting in a tree.' is ticked **Grammar essentials:** A subordinate clause (here 'As we walked through the woods') is introduced by a subordinating conjunction (here 'As'). It is dependent on a main clause (here 'we saw an owl sitting in a tree.') – it doesn't make sense on its own.	1
8	**Award 1 mark** for verbs written and spelled correctly in the simple past tense: While I **played** tennis yesterday, it **began** to rain. Mia **went** to Spain last summer. **Grammar essentials:** The simple past tense is used to talk about something that happened in the past and which has now finished.	1
9	**Award 1 mark** for brackets inserted correctly: We went to Paris **(**the capital city of France**)** for a long weekend. **Punctuation essentials:** Brackets can be used to indicate parenthesis. Information in parentheses is additional information.	1
10	**Award 1 mark** for 'mine' circled. **Grammar essentials:** A possessive pronoun refers to a person or thing that belongs to someone or something.	1
11	**Award 1 mark** for the insertion of 'carefully' or 'carelessly', spelled correctly. **Grammar essentials:** A suffix is a letter or string of letters that can be added to a word to turn it into another word.	1
12	**Award 1 mark** if the correct box is ticked: I am having cheese and cucumber sandwiches**,** a yoghurt and an apple. **Punctuation essentials:** Commas can be used to separate items in lists (but not before 'and').	1
	Total	12

Q	Mark scheme for Grammar and Punctuation Test 3	Marks
1	**Award 1 mark** if the sentence 'Are there any more books on the table' is ticked. **Grammar essentials:** A question is a sentence that asks something. It is followed by a question mark.	1
2	**Award 1 mark** for an appropriate adverb, spelled correctly. For example: The girls **quickly** worked out the answer. **Grammar essentials:** An adverb can say how something happens. Remember, not all adverbs end in 'ly' and not all words ending in 'ly' are adverbs!	1
3	**Award 1 mark** for correct positioning of inverted commas: **"**If you tidy your room, we will go to the park,**"** Bill's mum said. **Punctuation essentials:** Inverted commas come at the start and the end of direct speech. The final inverted comma must come after the final punctuation mark.	1
4	**Award 1 mark** if 'Bring your bike into the garage' is ticked. **Grammar essentials:** A command is a sentence that tells you to do something. The final punctuation can be a full stop or an exclamation mark.	1
5	**Award 1 mark** if both verbs are correct: is sitting, are running. **Grammar essentials:** The present progressive tense can describe events that are in progress/happening now.	1
6	**Award 1 mark** for 'has picked' ticked. **Grammar essentials:** The present perfect tense describes something that began in the past but may still continue into the present.	1
7	**Award 1 mark** if 'There is a new film on at the cinema.' is ticked. **Grammar essentials:** In Standard English, we use correct grammar.	1

Q	Mark scheme for Grammar and Punctuation Test 3	Marks
8	**Award 1 mark** for the word 'courageous' inserted and spelled correctly. **Grammar essentials:** A suffix is a letter or string of letters added to the end of one word to turn it into another word. An adjective can come before a noun, to modify it.	1
9	**Award 1 mark** for both 'down' and 'under' circled. **Grammar essentials:** A preposition links a noun, pronoun or noun phrase to another word in the sentence.	1
10	**Award 1 mark** if all are correct: contracted form, possession, contracted form, possession. **Punctuation essentials:** An apostrophe can be used to show the place of a missing letter or letters, or to show possession.	1
11	**Award 1 mark** for an appropriate noun phrase. For example: **Our old granddad** lives in a cottage by the sea. **Grammar essentials:** A noun phrase is a group of words that provides more information about a noun. The noun is the most important word in the phrase.	1
12	**Award 1 mark** if all are correct: it's, would've. **Grammar/punctuation essentials:** The apostrophes here are used to indicate exactly where letters have been removed as two words are contracted.	1
	Total	12

Q	Mark scheme for Grammar and Punctuation Test 4	Marks
1	**Award 1 mark** for correctly circling the conjunction in each sentence: **After** we had finished eating, we all helped to wash up. Beth likes tennis **but** she's not keen on badminton. The school caretaker was brushing up the leaves **as** we left school. **Grammar essentials:** A conjunction links two words or phrases together. Conjunctions can be either coordinating (linking two words or phrases together of equal importance) or subordinating (introducing a subordinate clause).	1
2	**Award 1 mark** if 'a statement' is ticked. **Grammar essentials:** A statement is a sentence that tells you something.	1
3	**Award 1 mark** if 'We are learning about World War I (also known as the Great War) in history.' is ticked. **Punctuation essentials:** Brackets can be used to indicate parenthesis. The words inside the brackets add extra information.	1
4	**Award 1 mark** if 'Dad switched the light off.' is ticked. **Grammar essentials:** Some words belong to more than one word class. The context of the sentence tells you whether these words are nouns, adjectives or verbs.	1
5	**Award 1 mark** for inserting the verb 'intensify', correctly spelled. **Grammar essentials:** Adding a suffix to a word can turn it into another word type, for example a verb, an adverb, a noun or an adjective.	1
6	**Award 1 mark** for all verbs correctly written: went, visited, saw. **Grammar essentials:** The simple past tense is used when we are talking about an event or situation in the past.	1
7	**Award 1 mark** for 'which' circled. **Grammar essentials:** The relative pronouns 'that', 'which', 'who', 'when', 'where' and 'whose' introduce a relative clause. They refer back to a noun or noun phrase that has come before.	1
8	**Award 1 mark** if 'We are going to the seaside today (unless it rains, of course).' is ticked. **Punctuation essentials:** Brackets can be used to indicate parenthesis. The words inside the brackets add extra information.	1
9	**Award 1 mark** for all the correct verbs circled: Ben and Joe done / **did** their maths homework together. Mum and I is / **are** going shopping later. There were / **was** a big storm during the night. **Grammar essentials:** In Standard English, we use correct grammar which includes subject-verb agreement.	1
10	**Award 1 mark** for both verbs correctly written: drove, preferred. **Grammar essentials:** The simple past tense is used when we are talking about an event or situation in the past.	1

Q	Mark scheme for Grammar and Punctuation Test 4	Marks
11	**Award 1 mark** for both commas correctly placed: After break**,** our teacher usually reads us a story. Today**,** the head teacher read to us instead. **Grammar essentials:** These sentences begin with fronted adverbials; they describe the action that follows and end with a comma.	1
12	**Award 1 mark** for the correct sentence ticked: Leah put the books on the shelf **Grammar essentials:** A preposition links a noun, pronoun or noun phrase to another word in the sentence.	1
	Total	12

Q	Mark scheme for Grammar and Punctuation Test 5	Marks
1	**Award 1 mark** for both adverbials circled: Later on, nearby. **Grammar essentials:** An adverb or adverbial can say how, when, how often or where something happens.	1
2	**Award 1 mark** if 'Mum, who was really handy, built a go-cart.' is ticked. **Grammar essentials:** The relative pronouns 'that', 'which', 'who', 'when', 'where' and 'whose' introduce a relative clause. They refer back to a noun or noun phrase that has come before.	1
3	**Award 1 mark** for all three correct: thankful, dangerous, temperamental. **Grammar essentials:** A suffix is a letter or string of letters added to the end of one word to turn it into another word, for example a verb, an adverb, a noun or an adjective.	1
4	**Award 1 mark** for 'Bavini's' circled. **Punctuation essentials:** An apostrophe can be used to show the place of a missing letter or letters.	1
5	**Award 1 mark** if 'What an amazing garden you have' is ticked. **Grammar essentials:** An exclamation sentence starts with 'what' or 'how', contains a verb (otherwise it wouldn't be a sentence!) and ends with an exclamation mark.	1
6	**Award 1 mark** for appropriate choice of verb tenses. For example: Sam always **eats/ate** his lunch with Hiro. Our friends went home after they **had watched/watched** the film. **Grammar essentials:** In English, tense is the choice between present and past verbs. It normally indicates differences of time.	1
7	**Award 1 mark** for the correct boxes ticked: There are lots of children in my dance class**,** 20 to be exact**,** and we all get along very well. **Punctuation essentials:** Commas can be used to indicate parenthesis (additional information), as well as to separate items in a list.	1
8	**Award 1 mark** for the addition of one word in the same word family. For example: circumnavigate, circuit, circumstance, circle. **Grammar essentials:** A word family is a group of words that share the same root.	1
9	**Award 1 mark** if all are correct: subordinate clause, main clause, subordinate clause. **Grammar essentials:** A subordinate clause is introduced by a subordinating conjunction. It is dependent on a main clause – it doesn't make sense on its own.	1
10	**Award 1 mark** if 'We had a boat trip on the River Thames.' is ticked. **Grammar essentials:** Proper nouns are the names of people, places, days of the week, months of the year, book and film titles. They start with a capital letter.	1
11	**a. Award 1 mark** for using <u>tie</u> as a verb. For example: I learned to tie my laces when I was five. **b. Award 1 mark** for using <u>tie</u> as a noun. For example: She has left her tie at school. **Grammar essentials:** Some words belong to more than one word class. The context of the sentence tells you whether these words are nouns, adjectives or verbs.	2
	Total	12

Q	Mark scheme for Grammar and Punctuation Test 6	Marks
1	**Award 1 mark** if 'Hand in your homework' is ticked. **Grammar essentials:** A command is a sentence that tells you to do something. It can end with a full stop or an exclamation mark.	1
2	**Award 1 mark** for punctuating the passage correctly: In the summer holidays, I like going to the seaside. **W**hile we are there, we usually visit my grandparents who have a caravan nearby. **I**t's even better if the sun is shining. **Punctuation essentials:** Full stops and capital letters are used to indicate the end of one sentence and the beginning of the next.	1
3	**Award 1 mark** for the correct verb form circled: Last week, we **climbed** / climb to the top of the hill. They usually **eat** / are eating cereal and toast for breakfast. Yesterday, I am swimming / **was swimming** in a competition. **Grammar essentials:** A verb must 'agree' with the subject in the sentence.	1
4	**Award 1 mark** for the word 'it'. Do not accept a capitalised 'i'. **Grammar essentials:** A pronoun replaces a noun, noun phrase or proper noun.	1
5	**Award 1 mark** for all three words spelled correctly: lovely, horribly, hungrily. **Grammar essentials:** A suffix is a letter or string of letters added to the end of one word to turn it into another word, for example a verb, an adverb or an adjective.	1
6	**Award 1 mark** for 'had tidied'. **Grammar essentials:** The past perfect tense describes an event that happened before something else took place. It is formed from the past tense of the verb 'to have' followed by the past participle of the main verb.	1
7	**Award 1 mark** if 'My sister Scarlet (who only yesterday stubbed her toe) has just fallen off the trampoline.' is ticked. **Punctuation essentials:** Brackets can be used to indicate parenthesis. The words inside brackets give additional information.	1
8	**Award 1 mark** for the correct sentence ticked: Mum's picking me up in her car. **Grammar essentials:** In Standard English, we use correct grammar which includes subject-verb agreement.	1
9	**Award 1 mark** for all correct: M, S, M. **Grammar essentials:** A subordinate clause (here 'which meant it was time to stop') is introduced by a subordinating conjunction (here 'which'). It is dependent on a main clause – it doesn't make sense on its own. A main clause makes sense on its own.	1
10	**Award 1 mark** if 'apostrophe' is ticked. **Grammar essentials:** An apostrophe can be used to show ownership or possession. If the noun is plural, the apostrophe comes after the final 's' (unless it is an irregular plural such as 'children', 'men' or 'women').	1
11	**a. Award 1 mark** if 'his' is underlined. **b. Award 1 mark** if 'Archie's pen' is ticked. **Grammar essentials:** A possessive pronoun refers to a person or thing that belongs to someone or something.	2
	Total	**12**

Q	Mark scheme for Grammar and Punctuation Test 7	Marks
1	**Award 1 mark** for a correctly punctuated sentence with no additional words: Is Bill walking his dog? **Grammar essentials:** A question is a sentence that asks something. It starts with a capital letter and ends with a question mark.	1
2	**Award 1 mark** if all correct: incorrectly, correctly, incorrectly, correctly. **Punctuation essentials:** When commas are used to separate items in a list, the first comma comes after the first list item. A pair of commas can be used to indicate parenthesis.	1
3	**Award 1 mark** for the relative clause underlined: The floods that followed the storms have destroyed many homes. **Grammar essentials:** A relative clause is a type of subordinate clause, introduced by a relative pronoun.	1
4	**Award 1 mark** for both words circled: has, win. **Grammar essentials:** In English, tense is the choice between present and past verbs.	1

Q	Mark scheme for Grammar and Punctuation Test 7	Marks
5	**Award I mark** for the word 'his'. **Grammar essentials:** A possessive pronoun refers to a person or thing that belongs to someone or something.	I
6	**Award I mark** if 'All over the world, there is evidence of dinosaur footprints.' is ticked. **Grammar essentials:** This sentence begins with a fronted adverbial. It describes an action that follows and it ends with a comma.	I
7	**Award I mark** if the word 'adjectives' is ticked. **Grammar essentials:** An adjective is used to describe and give more information about a noun.	I
8	**Award I mark** if both commas placed correctly: Mary, Jane thinks, is going to be late. **Punctuation essentials:** Commas can be used to avoid ambiguity/clarify meaning.	I
9	**Award I mark** if 'expanded noun phrase' is ticked. **Grammar essentials:** An expanded noun phrase is a noun phrase with additional information about the noun.	I
10	**Award I mark** if 'Gus ate his vegetables although he didn't really like them.' is ticked **Grammar essentials:** In English, tense is the choice between present and past verbs. It is important to be consistent in your choice of tense.	I
11	**Award I mark** for 're': **re**write **Grammar essentials:** A prefix is a group of letters added to the beginning of a word to turn it into another word. A prefix does not alter the spelling of the word it is joined to.	I
12	**Award I mark** for the word 'delicately', spelled correctly. **Grammar essentials:** A suffix is a letter or string of letters added to the end of one word to turn it into another word, for example, a verb, an adverb or an adjective.	I
	Total	12

Q	Mark scheme for Grammar and Punctuation Test 8	Marks
1	**Award I mark** for both conjunctions circled: and, but. **Grammar essentials:** Coordinating conjunctions such as 'and', 'but' and 'or' can link two words or phrases together.	I
2	**Award I mark** if all are correct. We have been learning about ancient Greece – statement What have you learned about ancient Greece – question What a lot we have learned about ancient Greece – exclamation Read this book about ancient Greece – command **Grammar essentials:** A command is a sentence that tells you to do something and ends with a full stop or an exclamation mark; a statement is a sentence that tells you something and ends with a full stop; a question is a sentence that asks something and ends with a question mark; an exclamation sentence starts with 'what' or 'how', contains a verb and ends with an exclamation mark.	I
3	**Award I mark** for a comma placed correctly: With only two minutes to go, it was clear who would win the race. **Grammar essentials:** A fronted adverbial is followed by a comma.	I
4	**Award I mark** if 'were driving' is ticked. **Grammar essentials:** The past progressive tense describes an event that was in progress.	I
5	**Award I mark** if the sentence 'There should be an apostrophe between the 'n' and the 's' in 'childrens'.' is ticked. **Punctuation essentials:** An apostrophe can be used to show ownership or possession. If the noun is plural, the apostrophe comes after the final 's', unless it is an irregular plural such as 'children', 'men' or 'women', in which case it comes after the word followed by 's'.	I
6	**Award I mark** if the subordinate clause is underlined: 'Remi did well in the maths test, <u>even though he found it difficult.</u>' **Grammar essentials:** A subordinate clause is introduced by a subordinating conjunction. It is dependent on the main clause – it does not make sense on its own.	I
7	**Award I mark** if all three are correct: classify, designate, advertise. **Grammar essentials:** A suffix is a letter or string of letters added to the end of one word to turn it into another word, for example, a verb, an adverb or an adjective.	I

Q	Mark scheme for Grammar and Punctuation Test 8	Marks
8	**Award I mark** if 'Joe's done lots of hard work today.' is ticked. **Grammar essentials:** In Standard English, we use correct grammar.	I
9	**Award I mark** if both are correct: luckily, hard. **Grammar essentials:** An adverb or adverbial can say when, how, how often or where something happens.	I
10	**Award I mark** if 'Mum's brother – the one who lives in South Africa – is staying with us for a fortnight.' is ticked. **Punctuation essentials:** Double dashes can be used to indicate parenthesis.	I
11	**Award I mark** if both verb forms correctly circled: There was/**were** lots of people waiting in the queue. They was / **were** cheering the winning team. **Grammar essentials:** The subject must agree with the verb in a sentence.	I
12	**Award I mark** for 'that' circled. **Grammar essentials:** A relative pronoun ('who', 'which', 'that', 'whose', 'where', 'when') introduces a relative clause.	I
	Total	12

Q	Mark scheme for Grammar and Punctuation Test 9	Marks
1	**Award I mark** if both are correct: Faye's, It's. **Punctuation essentials:** Apostrophes should only be used to show contraction (it is = it's) or to show where something belongs to someone or something (possession). Plural nouns on their own do not need an apostrophe.	I
2	**Award I mark** if all three determiners are circled: the, an, a. **Grammar essentials:** A determiner indicates whether a noun is specific/known or more general/unknown.	I
3	**Award I mark** for the addition of another word in the same word family, for example: really, realistic, realism. **Grammar essentials:** A word family is a group of words that share the same root.	I
4	**Award I mark** for the expanded forms, spelled correctly: I have, I am, it has **Punctuation essentials:** An apostrophe can be used to indicate a missing letter or letters.	I
5	**Award I mark** if 'How wonderful to see you at last' is ticked. **Grammar essentials:** An exclamation sentence starts with 'what' or 'how', contains a subject and a verb and ends with an exclamation mark.	I
6	**Award I mark** if 'I really admire the player who scored.' is ticked. **Grammar essentials:** In Standard English, we use correct grammar.	I
7	**Award I mark** for 'went'. **Grammar essentials:** The simple past tense is used when we are talking about an event or situation in the past.	I
8	**Award I mark** if 'In the middle of February, the daffodils' is ticked. **Grammar essentials:** A fronted adverbial is followed by a comma.	I
9	**Award I mark** if the correct homophone 'their' is circled. **Grammar essentials:** Homophones are words that sound the same but are spelled differently and have different meanings.	I
10	**Award I mark** for the word 'him' circled. **Grammar essentials:** A pronoun replaces a noun, proper noun or noun phrase.	I
11	**Award I mark** if 'a comma' is ticked. **Punctuation essentials:** A pair of commas can indicate parenthesis. The words outside the commas make sense on their own.	I
12	**Award I mark** for correctly writing the sentence with a comma: Although it was threatening to rain, we went for a picnic. **Grammar essentials:** A subordinating conjunction introduces a subordinate clause. A subordinate clause does not make sense on its own.	I
	Total	12

Q	Mark scheme for Grammar and Punctuation Test 10	Marks
1	**Award 1 mark** if 'which' is circled. **Grammar essentials:** A relative pronoun ('who', 'which', 'that', 'whose', 'where', 'when') introduces a relative clause. A relative clause is a type of subordinate clause that gives extra information about a noun previously mentioned in the sentence.	1
2	**Award 1 mark** if 'My cousin Sam (always full of determination and courage) climbed to the top of Mount Snowdon.' is ticked. **Punctuation essentials:** Brackets can indicate parenthesis. The words outside the brackets make sense on their own.	1
3	**Award 1 mark** if 'There are still some children <u>who have yet to finish</u>.' is ticked. **Grammar essentials:** A relative clause is introduced by a relative pronoun.	1
4	**Award 1 mark** if 'I shall visit my aunt at the weekend.' is ticked. **Grammar essentials:** The modal verb ('shall') shows how certain something is.	1
5	**Award 1 mark** for all correct: main clause, subordinate clause, main clause. **Grammar essentials:** A main clause makes sense on its own. A subordinate clause doesn't; it needs a main clause to make sense.	1
6	**Award 1 mark** for a correctly punctuated question with no additional words: Was Carmen late today? **Grammar essentials:** A question is a sentence that asks something. It starts with a capital letter and ends with a question mark.	1
7	**Award 1 mark** if the conjunction 'if' is circled. **Grammar essentials:** A subordinating conjunction introduces a subordinate clause. A subordinate clause does not make sense on its own.	1
8	**Award 1 mark** if '"Who is coming outside to play?" shouted Amir.' is circled. **Punctuation essentials:** The inverted commas in direct speech come before the opening speech and after the final punctuation mark of the speech.	1
9	**Award 1 mark** for all three correct: assistant, expectation, reference. **Grammar essentials:** A suffix is a letter or string of letters added to the end of one word to turn it into another word, for example a verb, a noun, an adverb or an adjective.	1
10	**Award 1 mark** if the correct conjunctions are inserted: There were baubles **and** lights on the tree, **but** Mum still hadn't added any tinsel **or** a fairy. **Grammar essentials:** Coordinating conjunctions such as 'and', 'but' and 'or' can link two words or phrases together.	1
11	**Award 1 mark** for two boxes ticked correctly: "Today we are going to investigate animal habitats and adaptation," our teacher said. **Grammar essentials:** The inverted commas in direct speech come before the opening speech and after the final punctuation mark of the speech.	1
12	**Award 1 mark** for an appropriate noun phrase. For example: Through his telescope, Finlay could see an incredibly bright light. **Grammar essentials:** A noun phrase is a group of words that provides more information about the noun in the phrase.	1
	Total	12

How to administer the spelling tests

There are ten short spelling tests in this book. Each test consists of four questions and should take approximately ten minutes to complete, although you should allow your child as much time as they need to complete them.

Read the instructions in the box below. The instructions are similar to the ones given in the National Curriculum tests. This will familiarise children with the style and format of the tests and show them what to expect.

> *Listen carefully to the instructions I am going to give you.*
>
> *I am going to read four sentences to you. Each sentence on your answer sheet has a missing word. Listen carefully to the missing word and write it in the space provided, making sure you spell the word correctly.*
>
> *I will read the word, then the word within the sentence, then repeat the word a third time.*
>
> *Do you have any questions?*

Read the spellings as follows:

- Give the question number, 'Spelling 1'
- Say, 'The word is...'
- Read the whole sentence to show the word in context
- Repeat, 'The word is...'

Leave at least a 12-second gap between each spelling.

At the end re-read all four questions. Then say, 'This is the end of the test. Please put down your pencil or pen.'

Each correct answer should be awarded **1 mark**.

Spelling test transcripts

Spelling test 1

Spelling 1: The word is **accompany**.
My teacher asked me to **accompany** her to the library.
The word is **accompany**.

Spelling 2: The word is **suggested**.
Mum **suggested** that we went to the park.
The word is **suggested**.

Spelling 3: The word is **programme**.
My favourite **programme** is on TV tonight.
The word is **programme**.

Spelling 4: The word is **competition**.
Padraig won the art **competition** in our class.
The word is **competition**.

Spelling test 2

Spelling 1: The word is **dictionary**.
Our teacher said we could use a **dictionary** to help us.
The word is **dictionary**.

Spelling 2: The word is **bruise**.
Freddy got a large **bruise** after he fell over.
The word is **bruise**.

Spelling 3: The word is **wary**.
We were very **wary** when we saw the bull in the field.
The word is **wary**.

Spelling 4: The word is **ancient**.
We have been looking at the **ancient** ruins of Pompeii.
The word is **ancient**.

Spelling test 3

Spelling 1: The word is **explanation**.
There was no **explanation** for the missing library book.
The word is **explanation**.

Spelling 2: The word is **restaurant**.
We went to a **restaurant** to celebrate Mum's birthday.
The word is **restaurant**.

Spelling 3: The word is **vegetables**.
I eat both fruit and **vegetables** to keep me healthy.
The word is **vegetables**.

Spelling 4: The word is **shoulder**.
Wahid banged his **shoulder** playing rugby.
The word is **shoulder**.

Spelling test 4

Spelling 1: The word is **excellent**.
Dad cooked an **excellent** stew.
The word is **excellent**.

Spelling 2: The word is **queue**.
The children waited for ages in the **queue**.
The word is **queue**.

Spelling 3: The word is **equipment**.
We took out the climbing **equipment** in PE today.
The word is **equipment**.

Spelling 4: The word is **committee**.
Florence is a member of the school safety **committee**.
The word is **committee**.

Spelling test transcripts

Spelling test 5

Spelling 1: The word is **marvellous**.
We had a **marvellous** trip to the farm.
The word is **marvellous**.

Spelling 2: The word is **occupation**.
My dad's **occupation** is firefighter.
The word is **occupation**.

Spelling 3: The word is **immediately**.
We **immediately** lined up when the alarm
sounded.
The word is **immediately**.

Spelling 4: The word is **their**.
Our parents are celebrating **their** wedding
anniversary.
The word is **their**.

Spelling test 6

Spelling 1: The word is **terrified**.
Dad was **terrified** he would scratch his new car.
The word is **terrified**.

Spelling 2: The word is **curious**.
There was a **curious** sound coming from
outside.
The word is **curious**.

Spelling 3: The word is **availability**.
Aunty Liz checked the **availability** of flights
to Ireland.
The word is **availability**.

Spelling 4: The word is **determined**.
I was **determined** to get my spellings correct.
The word is **determined**.

Spelling test 7

Spelling 1: The word is **important**.
It is **important** to eat a balanced diet.
The word is **important**.

Spelling 2: The word is **hurries**.
Ben **hurries** to open his birthday present.
The word is **hurries**.

Spelling 3: The word is **thorough**.
We gave the garage a **thorough** tidy.
The word is **thorough**.

Spelling 4: The word is **envelope**.
I put the invitation in a white **envelope**.
The word is **envelope**.

Spelling test 8

Spelling 1: The word is **preferred**.
Petra **preferred** PE on the playing field.
The word is **preferred**.

Spelling 2: The word is **neighbour**.
Our **neighbour** has two dogs and a cat.
The word is **neighbour**.

Spelling 3: The word is **forty**.
Mum is **forty** next year.
The word is **forty**.

Spelling 4: The word is **castle**.
We visited the medieval **castle** on the hill.
The word is **castle**.

Spelling test transcripts

Spelling test 9

Spelling 1: The word is **transferred**.
Dad has been **transferred** to a different factory.
The word is **transferred**.

Spelling 2: The word is **tough**.
Our last spelling test was **tough** but fair.
The word is **tough**.

Spelling 3: The word is **island**.
The yacht sailed towards the **island** in the distance.
The word is **island**.

Spelling 4: The word is **ceiling**.
We watched the spider crawl across the **ceiling**.
The word is **ceiling**.

Spelling test 10

Spelling 1: The word is **mischievous**.
The **mischievous** little puppy chewed Mum's slippers.
The word is **mischievous**.

Spelling 2: The word is **occupied**.
Jim was **occupied** with his science experiment.
The word is **occupied**.

Spelling 3: The word is **bargain**.
We always get a **bargain** in the January sales.
The word is **bargain**.

Spelling 4: The word is **exaggerates**.
Mo sometimes **exaggerates** how hungry he is.
The word is **exaggerates**.

Progress chart

Fill in your score in the table below
to see how well you've done.

Test number (Grammar, Punctuation and Spelling)	Score
Test 1	
Test 2	
Test 3	
Test 4	
Test 5	
Test 6	
Test 7	
Test 8	
Test 9	
Test 10	
TOTAL	

Mark	
0–50	Good try! You need more practice in some topics – ask an adult to help you.
51–110	You're doing really well. Ask for extra help for any topics you found tricky.
111–160	You're a 10-Minute SATs Test grammar, punctuation and spelling star – good work!

Reward Certificate

Well done!

*You have completed all of the
10-Minute SATs Tests*

Name: _____   Date: _____

QUICK TESTS FOR SATs SUCCESS

BOOST YOUR CHILD'S CONFIDENCE WITH 10-MINUTE SATs TESTS

- Bite-size mini SATs tests which take just 10 minutes to complete
- Covers key National Test topics
- Full answers and progress chart provided to track improvement
- Available for Years 1 to 6